Hands Sing the Blues

Romare Bearden's Childhood Journey

by

Jeanne Walker Harvey

illustrated by

Elizabeth Zunon

Marshall Cavendish Children

Special thanks to Uma Krishnaswami, teacher extraordinaire, and Margery Cuyler,
editor extraordinaire, and the SFMOMA Docent Program

Painting on page 5: art © Romare Bearden Foundation/Licensed by VAGA, New York, NY
The Romare Bearden Foundation, a New York based nonprofit organization established in 1990,
preserves, perpetuates and makes publicly accessible Romare Bearden's rich artistic and intellectual legacy through its programs.
Beyond the material legacy, which includes his art, archives and literary works, the Foundation has built its
programmatic mission on Bearden's legacy of nurturing and supporting the creative and intellectual
potential of artists, children and scholars (www.beardenfoundation.org).

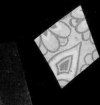

Text copyright © 2011 by Jeanne Walker Harvey
Illustrations copyright © 2011 by Elizabeth Zunon
All rights reserved
Marshall Cavendish Corporation, 99 White Plains Road, Tarrytown, NY 10591
www.marshallcavendish.us/kids

Library of Congress Cataloging-in-Publication Data
Harvey, Jeanne Walker.
My hands sing the blues / by Jeanne Walker Harvey ; illustrated by
Elizabeth Zunon. — 1st ed.
p. cm.
Summary: In Harlem, New York City, an artist follows the rhythms of blues
music as he recalls his North Carolina childhood while painting, cutting,
and pasting to make art.
ISBN 978-0-7614-5810-4   e-books ISBN 978-0-7614-6063-3
[1. Stories in rhyme. 2. Artists—Fiction. 3. Blues (Music)—Fiction. 4.
North Carolina—Fiction. 5. Harlem (New York, N.Y.)—Fiction.] I. Zunon,
Elizabeth, ill. II. Title.
PZ8.3.H258713My 2010
[E]—dc22
2010016849

The illustrations are rendered in oil paint with mixed media collage.
Book design by Anahid Hamparian
Editor: Margery Cuyler

Printed in China (E)
First edition
1 3 5 6 4 2

mc **Marshall Cavendish**
Children

For my mother, June, who always inspires me to put a beat of color on an empty canvas
—J.W.H.

For my family and my memories of home
—E.Z.

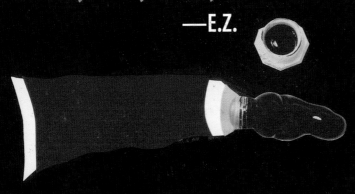

"You put down one color, and it calls for an answer. You have to look at it like a melody."
—Romare Bearden

I SNIP A PATCH OF COLOR and add a cut-out face.
Oh! I glue on jazzy blue for sky and add another face.
People walk into my work as if it's always been their place.

My hands sing the blues when I paint and cut and paste.
I never know what I'll create when I paint and cut and paste.
I use paper, fabrics, photos, and nothing goes to waste.

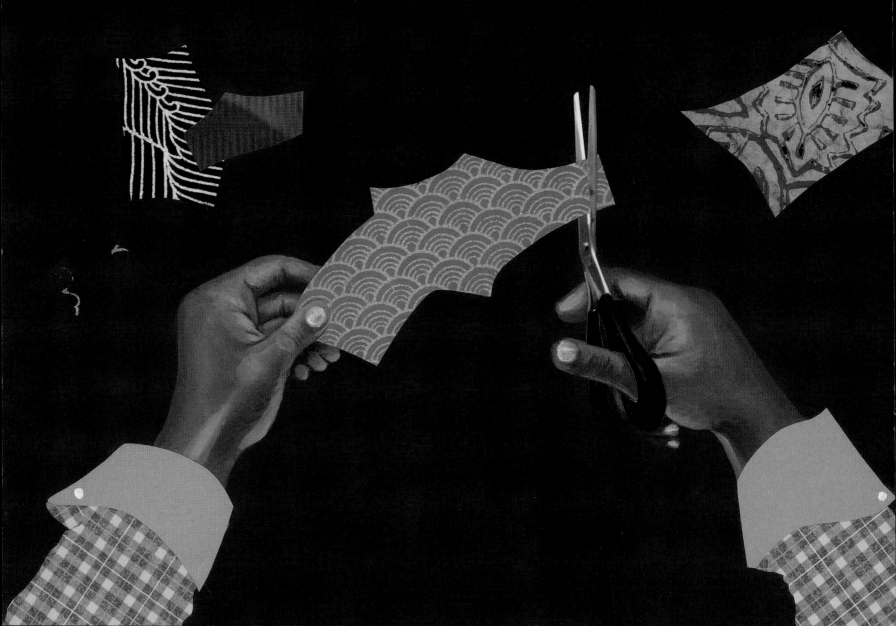

Today my memory whirls back to my North Carolina past.
Swirling days of hot July, picking berries in my past.
Just then a train roars across my canvas with a loud and steamy blast.

I'm back as a boy, talking with Great-grandma down the old dirt road.
I'm walking with Great-grandma down the old dirt road
to the land of the Cherokees from where her stories flowed.

Rocking on her creaky swing, we hear the crickets chirp.
We feel the humming of Magnolia Mill and hear the crickets chirp.
We gulp down warm tomato slices, trying not to slurp.

Riding up on Great-grandpa's shoulders, I'm a strong and mighty tower.
My chin resting on his head, I'm a strong and mighty tower.
We're watching the good trains go by hour after hour.

We know every train by its swinging whistle tune.
Each engineer plays a different whistle tune,
like the Atlanta-New York Special sizzling through at noon.

The trains *cha-chunk cha-chunk* on by. WHOO-WHOOO WHOO-WHOOO
One more round of whistles. *WHOO-WHOOO WHOO-WHOOO*
WHAH-WHAH DE-DOO WHURR-WHURR DE-WHURR

WHAH-WHAH DE-DOOO

Then one day I'm waiting on a bench for a train to roll on in.
Mom and Pop and me, we're waiting for a train to roll on in
to take us to New York, where our new life will begin.

From the South to the North, many more have gone before me.
Riding on the railroads, many more have gone before me,
wanting to be free like the wind blows through a tree.

From somewhere down the track, I can hear that whistle blow.

I tap my toes to the beat and hear that whistle blow.

WHOA-DE-WHOA

The locomotive slides in slow.

Lifting luggage up the stairs, the Pullman porter nods at us.
Standing by the sleeping cars, the Pullman porter smiles at us.
But we can't go in the sleeping cars, and we're not to make a fuss.

Tears sting my eyes when I hear the call, "All aboard!"
I hug Great-grandma and Great-grandpa, then I climb aboard.
I settle in my seat and wonder what we're traveling toward.

TINK-A-TINK TINK-A-TINK The engine picks up speed. *KA-NOOK KA-NEE*

TINK-A-TINK TINK-A-TINK Bye-bye, Trade Street Station.

KA-NOOK KA-NEE

With a-thrumming and a-drumming, the train hums a tune to me.

I press my nose against the glass and watch the world whizzing by.
A patchwork quilt of greens and golds, the world whizzing by.
Farms and fields of cotton. Roosters pecking bugs nearby.

I spy a woman by a washtub, stirring, staring up at me.
I wonder what she's thinking, staring up at me.
Maybe that tomorrow so far away I'll be.

The train **ga-glides ga-glides** us up to Harlem, New York City.
That's where I am right now, painting what's inside of me,
sharing stories of my past and the joys and fears inside of me.

Like a flower, I have roots in my Carolina past,
roots sunk deep in my childhood long past.
The people and the places are in my art to last.

When I begin something new, I take it slow and steady.
I let myself become my art and take it slow and steady.
I'll lag behind the beat until I'm sure I'm ready.

I want my art to touch each of us so we can understand.
I want to follow roads from secret places so we can understand
that the blues sing for each of us all across the land.

I'm like a singer calling out, then holding back.
I'm like a trumpet player blowing loud, then dropping back.
When I put a beat of color on an empty canvas,
   I never know what's coming down the track.

AUTHOR'S NOTE

After the Civil War, Romare Bearden's great-grandparents were among the African-American middle class that established businesses in Charlotte, Mecklenburg County, North Carolina, where the railroad and cotton industries prospered. When Bearden was a young child, however, his family faced discriminatory Jim Crow laws and attitudes. In 1914, the three-year-old Bearden and his college-educated parents participated in the Great Migration North, moving to New York City. After his family moved to Harlem, Bearden spent many fondly remembered summer vacations in North Carolina with his great-grandparents.

Bearden, of African, Cherokee, and Italian descent, was one of America's most vibrant and innovative 20th-century artists. Although Bearden achieved artistic success with different styles and media, today he's remembered mainly for his collages, which he referred to as "paintings." In his collages, he not only analyzed the social and political issues of his time, but he also told his personal story and the daily life experiences of African Americans living in the rural South and the urban North. In addition, his paintings incorporated references to music, classical art, literature, and religion. He described his process in creating these collages as follows:

"I first put down several rectangles of color some of which...are in the same ratio as...the rectangle that I'm working on. [Then] I paste a photograph, say, anything just to get me started, maybe a head, at certain...places in the canvas....I try to move up and across the canvas, always moving up and across." (Fine, Ruth. *The Art of Romare Bearden* [Washington, DC: National Gallery of Art, 2003], excerpt, 46)

Bearden had a passion for trains. He spent many hours as a boy with his great-grandfather watching trains roll through Charlotte. He included trains in some of his paintings to symbolize not only Charlotte and Pittsburgh, where his maternal grandmother lived, but also the Underground Railroad and the Great Migration to the North. My text was inspired by Bearden's painting, "Watching the Good Trains Go By," painted in 1964 and found here on page 5.

Romare Bearden died of complications from bone cancer on March 12, 1988, at the age of seventy-six. In his obituary in *The New York Times*, he was described as "one of America's preeminent artists" and "the nation's foremost collagist." He received many awards, including the National Medal of Arts, presented by President Ronald Reagan in 1987. He also dedicated himself to helping young, emerging artists.

I loosely based my text on the concept of the blues—all three lines rhyming, two lines incorporating similar end phrasing, and a variation in rhythm. I chose this form because Romare Bearden's art and life were inspired by blues and jazz music. W.C. Handy, the "Father of the Blues," brought the music of rural Southern African Americans into the mainstream during the 1910s and 1920s when Bearden was a young man. In addition, Bearden was influenced heavily by the world of jazz during the Harlem Renaissance. He often commented on the similarities between how he created his collages and how jazz musicians improvised. He called his paintings "visual jazz."

SOURCE NOTES

I am especially indebted to Ruth Fine for her exceptional book, *The Art of Romare Bearden*, published in conjunction with the National Gallery of Art's Bearden retrospective in 2003. As I led school groups on tours of the San Francisco Museum of Modern Art during the Bearden retrospective in 2004, I also learned a great deal about his work.

I've incorporated some of Romare Bearden's phrases and ideas into the text. The following quotes were lifted from Brown, Kevin. *Romare Bearden*. New York: Chelsea House, 1995:

Like a jazz musician, "you do something, and then you improvise" (p. 16)

"Once you get going all sorts of things open up." Sometimes things just seem "to fall into place, like the piano keys that seem to be right where your fingers come down." (pp. 16-17)

"I don't 'do' a collage. I just allow some of the people I know to come into the room." (p. 17)

When he switched from abstract painting to collage, "people started coming into my work, like opening a door." (p. 83)

"Most artists take some place, and like a flower, they sink roots. My roots are in North Carolina. I paint what people did when I was a little boy, like the way they got up in the morning." (p. 103)

"I never left Charlotte except physically." (p. 99)

About the trains that he watched for hours that were traveling through Charlotte: "You could tell not only the train but also who the engineer was—just by the whistle." (pp. 29-30)

"I think the artist has to be something like a whale, swimming with his mouth wide open, absorbing everything, until he has what he really needs. When he finds that, he can start to make limitations. And then he really begins to grow." (p. 79)

FOR MORE INFORMATION

Books

Fine, Ruth and Stewart, Frank (photographer). *Romare Bearden*. San Francisco: Pomegranate Communications, 2004.

Greenberg, Jan. *Romare Bearden: Collage of Memories*. New York: Harry N. Abrams, Inc., 2003.

Hartfield, Claire and Lagarrigue, Jerome (illustrator). *Me and Uncle Romie: A Story Inspired by the Life and Art of Romare Bearden*. New York: Dial Books, 2002.

Hughes, Langston and Bearden, Romare (illustrator). *The Block*. New York: Metropolitan Museum of Art, 1995.

Schwartzman, Myron. *Romare Bearden: Celebrating the Victory*. New York: Franklin Watts, 1999.

Video/DVD

The Art of Romare Bearden. National Gallery of Art, 2004. Produced, written, and directed by Carroll Moore.

Internet Sources

www.beardenfoundation.org (Romare Bearden Foundation)

www.sfmoma.org/bearden (San Francisco Museum of Modern Art)

www.nga.gov/feature/bearden/index.shtm (National Gallery of Art)

www.metmuseum.org/explore/the_block/index_flash.html (Metropolitan Museum)

www.aaa.si.edu/collectionsonline/bearroma/ (Smithsonian Archives of American Art – papers of Romare Bearden)